Angular for Beginners

Everything you need to know

Abdelfattah Ragab

Angular for Beginners

Everything you need to know

Abdelfattah Ragab

Introduction

Welcome to the book "Angular for beginners".
In this book, I'll tell you all about Angular in a free discussion format.
What is Angular, how can you build a real application with it and what are all the terms you hear every day like pipes, interceptors, lazy loading and so on.
You will learn everything in a few minutes and have a good understanding of what Angular can do and how you can use it for your applications. By the end of this book, you will realize that Angular is so easy, and you will be interested in moving on and creating your own Angular applications.
Let's get started.

Move forward

When you start a new topic, you should explore it broadly and focus on moving forward without getting lost in the details. I also recommend that you gather information on the same topic from different sources. Take breaks from time to time, look for short answers to questions, and use different sources to get different perspectives. Don´t worry if you still don't understand after many attempts, just keep going because you will come across it again later.

What is Angular?

Angular is a web framework that empowers developers to build fast, reliable applications. Maintained by a dedicated team at Google, Angular provides a broad suite of tools, APIs, and libraries to simplify and streamline your development workflow. Angular gives you a solid platform on which to build fast, reliable applications that scale with both the size of your team and the size of your codebase.

How to use Angular to create real life applications?

You use Angular to create components, connect them together and deploy the application online. It's like building block toys.

How do you organize your Angular application?

The most important building block in Angular is the component. When you connect your component to a route, it becomes a page.
If you use it within another component, it becomes a shared component.
You can create a "Layout" folder and store the components of Header, Footer, Sidenav and so on in it.

You can create another folder "Components" and place the common components such as product card, rating etc. in it.
You can create another folder "Pages" and store the components for products, shopping cart, about, contact etc. in it.
You can create folders for all kinds of artifacts such as "Pipes", "Guards", "Interceptors", "Services", "Directives" and so on.

What is Angular CLI?

Angular CLI is an easy way to create all artifacts like components, services, guards and so on.
Open the terminal and run the commands:

```
ng g c pages/about
```
Creates the "about" component in the pages folder

```
ng g s services/products
```
Creates the "products" service in the services folder

```
ng g p pipes/truncate
```
Creates the "truncate" pipe in the pipes folder

What is the Angular component?

An Angular component is a fundamental building block of an Angular application. It encapsulates a part of the user interface (UI) and defines how this part of the application behaves. Each component consists of three main parts:

Component class: This is a TypeScript class that contains the logic for the component.

Template: The template is an HTML file that defines the view for the component.

Metadata: Metadata is provided with the @Component decorator, which tells Angular how to process the component. This includes information such as the component's selector (the HTML tag used to embed the component), the path to the template and the styles associated with the component

Here's an example of what the products.component.ts file might look like:

```typescript
import { Component } from
'@angular/core';

@Component({
  selector: 'app-products,
  templateUrl:
'./products.component.html',
  styleUrls:
['./products.component.css']
```

```
})
export class ProductsComponent {


}
```

To generate it you need to execute the command
```
ng g c pages/products
```

Under the pages folder you will find the products folder
component and it will have the following files:
- `products.component.html`: The HTML
  template for the component.
- `products.component.css`: The CSS styles
  for the component.
- `products.component.ts`: The TypeScript file
  that defines the component class.
- `products.component.spec.ts`: The unit
  test file for the component.

Events

In the html template you write normal html code in which
you can use div, input, button and so on.
For each element you can handle events by defining the
name of the handler method. In the Typescript class,
you define the logic of the handler.
In the html:
```
<button (click)='onClick()" ></button>
```

In the TypeScript class:

```
onClick() {
    console.log('Clicked');
}
```

Routing

Angular routing allows you to manage the navigation and rendering of different views or components based on the current URL.
The key concepts are:
Routes: Routes are defined as an array of objects, where each object specifies a path and the corresponding component to be displayed when accessing this path. Usually it is defined in a file called *app.routes.ts*

```
import { Routes } from
'@angular/router';
import { AboutComponent } from
'./pages/about/about.component';
import { ProductsComponent } from
'./pages/products/products.component';

export const routes: Routes = [
  { path: 'about', component:
AboutComponent },
  { path: 'products', component:
ProductsComponent },
];
```

When you type the '/about' path in the address bar, the browser will display the AboutComponent.

Router Outlet: The `<router-outlet>` directive acts as a placeholder where the routed component will be displayed.

For example I can define the app.component.html as follows:

```
<app-header></app-header>
<div class='main'>
  <router-outlet/>
</div>
<app-footer></app-footer>
```

Component Lifecycle

A component's lifecycle is the sequence of steps that happen between the component's creation and its destruction.

The components go through four phases: Creation, change detection, rendering, and destruction.

The creation has only one method, the constructor, and the destruction also has only one method, namely ngOnDestroy.

Creation is followed by the change detection phase, which begins with the ngOnInit method.

The ngOnInit method is executed exactly once before the component's own template is initialized. This means that you can update the state of the component based on its initial input values.

The ngOnDestroy method is executed once, just before a component is destroyed. Angular destroys a component when it is no longer displayed on the page, e.g. when it is hidden by NgIf or when you navigate to another page.
If you have created any subscriptions or memory-intensive resources, you should delete them here before the component is destroyed to avoid memory loss.

Forms

Angular offers forms for processing user input. They are called Reactive Forms
There is an old way, Template Driven Forms, which does not scale well and is limited in its capabilities, so let us use the Reactive Forms.
Here is an example for a login form. It has an email and password input fields.
So the form will be:

```
    this.form = this.fb.group({
      email: this.fb.control('',
[Validators.required]),
      password: this.fb.control('',
[Validators.required]),
    });
```

Here is the full code of the component

```
import { Component, OnInit } from
'@angular/core';
```

```typescript
import {
  FormGroup,
  FormBuilder,
  ReactiveFormsModule,
  Validators,
} from '@angular/forms';

@Component({
  selector: 'app-login',
  standalone: true,
  imports: [ReactiveFormsModule],
  templateUrl: './login.component.html',
  styleUrl: './login.component.css',
})
export class LoginComponent implements
OnInit {
  form!: FormGroup;

  constructor(private readonly fb:
FormBuilder) {}

  ngOnInit(): void {
    this.form = this.fb.group({
      email: this.fb.control('',
[Validators.required]),
      password: this.fb.control('',
[Validators.required]),
    });
  }

  onSubmit() {
```

```
      console.log(this.form.value);
  }
}
```

In the html we connect the html form to the reactive form as follows. Here is the full html code:

```html
<form [formGroup]="form"
(ngSubmit)="onSubmit()">
  <input type="email"
formControlName="email" />
  <input type="password"
formControlName="password" />
  <button type="submit">Login</button>
</form>
```

First we have to connect the [formGroup] object. For all form fields, we need to specify the name of the form control by setting the formControlName.
No events are assigned to the button, but since it is of type submit, it will trigger the form submit event, which calls the onSubmit method handler.

Dependency Injection

"DI" is a design pattern and mechanism for creating and delivering some parts of an app to other parts of an app that require them.
As a developer, you should avoid writing business login into the components. You should move it to a separate service file.

Service is a broad category encompassing any value,
function, or feature that an application needs. A service
is typically a class with a narrow, well-defined purpose.
To create a service, execute the command:

```
ng g s services/auth
```

This will create the auth service inside the services
folder. I will define the login method inside the auth
service.

```
import { Injectable } from
'@angular/core';

@Injectable({
  providedIn: 'root',
})
export class AuthService {
  constructor() {}

  login(email: string, password: string)
{}
}
```

To use it in the login component you need first to inject it
in the constructor as follows

```
  constructor(
    private readonly fb: FormBuilder,
    private authService: AuthService
  ) {}
```

The constructor now has two services injected and one
of them is the AuthService.

Now we can use it in the onSubmit() method as follows:

```
onSubmit() {
    console.log(this.form.value);
```

```
this.authService.login(this.form.value.email, this.form.value.password);
    }
```

HTTP Client

Most front-end applications need to communicate with a server via the HTTP protocol to download or upload data and access other back-end services. Angular provides a client HTTP API for Angular applications, the HttpClient service.
To configure it go to app.config.ts and add to the providers array:

```
provideHttpClient(
        withFetch(),
    ),
```

Call the login method in the authService and use the http client to connect to the backend. Inject the http client into the constructor and use it in the login method. Here it is

```
import { HttpClient } from '@angular/common/http';
import { Injectable } from '@angular/core';
```

```typescript
@Injectable({
  providedIn: 'root',
})
export class AuthService {
  constructor(private readonly http:
HttpClient) {}

  login(email: string, password: string)
{
    return
this.http.post('https://backend.com/api/a
uth', {
      email,
      password,
    });
  }
}
```

Http client serivce returns observables. You must
subscribe to the observables in order for them to be
executed. Observables without subscribers are not
executed, as it makes no sense to execute an
observable that does not interest anyone who wants to
hear the results.

Go to the login component and subscribe to the login
method as follows

```typescript
onSubmit() {
    console.log(this.form.value);
    this.authService
```

```
      .login(this.form.value.email,
this.form.value.password)
      .pipe(first())
      .subscribe((response: any) => {
        console.log(response);
      });
  }
```

You can use operators before the subscribe method. In
this case, I use the first() operator to complete the
subscription after receiving the first result. Each time the
user clicks the subscribe button, a subscription is
created, the results are read and the subscription is
completed after the first result is read.

Environment variables

In the last example we made a little mistake, we hard
coded the backend url.
Angular environment variables are a way to manage
configuration settings for different environments (such
as development, staging, and production) in an Angular
application. They allow developers to define variables
that can change based on the environment in which the
application is running, making it easier to manage
settings like API endpoints, feature flags, and other
configuration options without hardcoding them into the
application.

To add environments to your application, execute the command:

```
ng g environments
```

In the environments folder you will find the environment files. Add a new entry to the apiUrl as follows

```
export const environment = {
  apiUrl: 'https://backend.com/api/',
};
```

Now we can use it in the authService. Update the login method as follows:

```
login(email: string, password: string) {
    return
this.http.post(environment.apiUrl +
'auth', {
      email,
      password,
    });
  }
```

Don't forget to import environment at the top of your file

```
import { environment } from
'../../environments/environment.developm
ent';
```

Guards

Angular Guards are interfaces that allow you to control access to routes in an Angular application. They are used to determine whether a user can navigate to a specific route or leave a route, providing a way to implement authentication, authorization, and other navigation-related logic.

You may have some protected pages in your application that should only be accessible to logged-in users.
To do this, go to the app.routes.ts file and add the canActivate method to the path you want to protect.

```
{ path: 'orders', component: OrdersComponent, canActivate: [authGuard] },
```

Here is an example on how the authGuard may look like

```
import { CanActivateFn, Router } from '@angular/router';
import { AuthService } from '../services/auth.service';
import { inject } from '@angular/core';

export const authGuard: CanActivateFn = (route, state) => {
  const authService = inject(AuthService);
  const router = inject(Router);
  if (authService.user.getValue())
return true;
  else return router.navigate(['/', 'login']);
};
```

if authService.user has the value, the user is allowed to visit the order page, otherwise he is redirected to the login page.

There is also the canDeactivate method to prevent the user from leaving the page in some cases, e.g. when changes are not saved.

Interceptors

Interceptors are generally functions that you can run for each request, and have wide-ranging capabilities to influence the content and overall flow of requests and responses. You can install multiple interceptors that form an interceptor chain, in which each interceptor processes the request or response before passing it on to the next interceptor in the chain.
After the first successful login, you will receive an access token from the backend. You must include this token in all outbound API requests.
To use the interceptor, update the provideHttpClient in the app.config.ts as follows

```
provideHttpClient(withInterceptors([authI
nterceptor]), withFetch()),
```

Here is how the interceptor looks like:
```
import { HttpInterceptorFn } from
'@angular/common/http';
import { inject } from '@angular/core';
```

```typescript
import { AuthService } from
'../services/auth.service';

export const authInterceptor:
HttpInterceptorFn = (req: any, next:
any) => {
  const authService =
inject(AuthService);
  const authReq = req.clone({
    headers:
req.headers.set('Authorization', 'Bearer
' + authService.token),
  });
  console.log('interceptor - auth
headers: ', authReq.headers);
  return next(authReq);
};
```

Resolvers

Angular Resolvers are a feature in Angular's routing module that allows you to prefetch data before a route is activated. This ensures that the necessary data is available to the component when it is loaded, improving the user experience by preventing loading states or empty views.

Create the resolver function that will fetch the data from the backend as follows

```typescript
import { inject } from '@angular/core';
```

```typescript
import { ResolveFn } from
'@angular/router';
import { OrdersService } from
'../services/orders.service';

export const ordersResolver:
ResolveFn<any> = (route, state) => {
  const ordersService =
inject(OrdersService);
  return ordersService.getOrders();
};
```

Go to the app.routes.ts and use revolver with the orders
path entry as follows:

```typescript
    {
      path: 'orders',
      component: OrdersComponent,
      canActivate: [authGuard],
      resolve: {
        orders: ordersResolver,
      },
    },
```

In the orders component init, we can read the orders
data as follows:

```typescript
import { Component } from
'@angular/core';
import { ActivatedRoute } from
'@angular/router';

@Component({
```

```typescript
  selector: 'app-orders',
  standalone: true,
  imports: [],
  templateUrl:
'./orders.component.html',
  styleUrl: './orders.component.css',
})
export class OrdersComponent {
  orders: any;

  constructor(private route:
ActivatedRoute) {}

  ngOnInit() {

this.route.data.subscribe((resolvedData:
any) => {
      this.orders = resolvedData.orders;
    });
  }
}
```

Lazy loading

Angular Lazy Loading is a design pattern that allows you
to load components on demand instead of loading the
entire application in advance. This technique is
particularly beneficial for optimizing the performance of
large Angular applications, as it reduces the initial load
time and improves the overall user experience.

This is the syntax for the eager loading as you already know:

```
    { path: 'orders', component:
OrdersComponent },
```

To lazy load a component change it to this:

```
    {
       path: 'orders',
       loadComponent: () =>

import('./pages/orders/orders.component')
.then((c) => c.OrdersComponent),
    },
```

This way, Angular will not download the javascript file of this component when the application starts. Later, when the user decides to visit the orders page, the javascript of this component will be downloaded.

Template syntax

In Angular, a *template* is a chunk of HTML. We use special syntax within a template to build on many of Angular's features.

For example, if we have a variable defined in the Typescript class whose value we want to display in the HTML template, we use the following double curly brackets as delimiters {{ and }}.

Say we have the variable price, we display it in the html as follows:

```
<div>{{ price }}</div>
```

This is called **text interpolation.**
You can bind to an html property. Say we have an html image tag and we want to set the src attribute to the value from the variable imageUrl from the TypeScript
To bind to an element's property, enclose it in square brackets, [], which identifies the property as a target property.

```
<img [src]='imageUrl' />
```

This is called **property binding.**

Pipes

Angular Pipes are a powerful feature in Angular that allows you to transform data for display in templates. They are essentially functions that take an input value, process it, and return a transformed output. Pipes are commonly used to format data, such as dates, currencies, or strings, making it easier to present information in a user-friendly manner.
There are built-in pipes to format numbers, for example. Suppose we have a variable price that we want to display in the form of two digits

```
{{ price | number : '1.2-2' }}
```

We can create custom pipes. Let's create a truncate pipe to limit the text displayed.
Execute the command:

```
ng g p pipes/truncate
```

Here it is:

```typescript
import { Pipe, PipeTransform } from
'@angular/core';

@Pipe({
  name: 'truncate',
  standalone: true,
})
export class TruncatePipe implements
PipeTransform {
  transform(
    value: string,
    limit: number = 100,
    ellipsis: string = '...'
  ): string {
    if (value.length <= limit) {
      return value;
    }
    return value.substring(0, limit) +
ellipsis;
  }
}
```

Now we can use it simply as follows:

```html
  <div class="title">{{ product.title |
truncate : 60 }}</div>
```

Don't forget to import it first

```typescript
import { TruncatePipe } from
'../../pipes/truncate.pipe';
```

```
@Component({
  selector: 'app-product-card',
  standalone: true,
  imports: [RatingComponent,
TruncatePipe],
  templateUrl:
'./product-card.component.html',
  styleUrl:
'./product-card.component.css',
})
export class ProductCardComponent {
```

Control flow

Angular templates support control flow blocks that let you conditionally show, hide, and repeat elements.

There is @if, @for and @switch

For example:

```
@if (user) {
  <div class="account">Welcome, {{
user.fullname }}</div>
} @else {
  <div class="login"
routerLink="/login">Login</div>
}
```

Styles

Each component has its own styles file in which you can define component-specific styles.
There is a global styles.css file that influences the styles of the entire application.

Data types

Number: Represents both integer and floating-point numbers. For example:

```
let age: number = 30;
let price: number = 19.99;
```

String: Used for textual data. Strings can be defined using single quotes, double quotes, or backticks for template literals. For example:

```
let name: string = 'John Doe';
let greeting: string = `Hello,
${name}!`;
```

Boolean: Represents a true/false value. For example:

```
let isActive: boolean = true;
```

Null and Undefined: These types represent the absence of a value. They can be explicitly assigned to variables:

```
let notAssigned: null = null;
let uninitialized: undefined;
```

Any: A special type that allows a variable to hold any type of value. It is useful when the type is not known at compile time:

```typescript
let randomValue: any = 42; // can be a
number, string, etc.
```

Array: A collection of values of a specific type. You can define an array using the type followed by square brackets:

```typescript
let numbers: number[] = [1, 2, 3, 4, 5];
let names: Array<string> = ['Alice',
'Bob', 'Charlie'];
```

Tuple: An array with a fixed number of elements where each element can have a different type:

```typescript
let user: [string, number] = ['Alice',
25];
```

Object: Represents a collection of key-value pairs. You can define an object type using an interface or directly:

```typescript
interface User {
  name: string;
  age: number;
}

let user: User = { name: 'Alice', age:
25 };
```

Enum: A way to define a set of named constants. Enums can be numeric or string-based:

```typescript
enum Color {
```

```typescript
  Red,
  Green,
  Blue
}

let favoriteColor: Color = Color.Green;
```

Void: Represents the absence of a type, commonly used for functions that do not return a value:

```typescript
function logMessage(message: string):
void {
  console.log(message);
}
```

Never: Indicates a value that never occurs, often used for functions that throw errors or have infinite loops:

```typescript
function throwError(message: string):
never {
  throw new Error(message);
}
```

Observables

Observables represent a stream of data that can be observed over time. In Angular, observables are commonly used for handling events, HTTP requests, and other asynchronous operations. For example, the Angular HttpClient service returns observables, allowing developers to subscribe to the results of HTTP calls.

RxJS

RxJS, or Reactive Extensions for JavaScript, is a powerful library that utilizes observables to manage asynchronous data flows, making it easier to compose and manage complex asynchronous operations.

Operators

RxJS provides a rich set of operators that allow developers to manipulate and transform data emitted by observables. Operators such as map, filter, mergeMap, and combineLatest enable developers to create complex data flows and handle various scenarios in a declarative manner.

Conclusion

Congratulations! You have completed the book "Angular for Beginners". Now you should have a solid understanding of what Angular is and how you can use it to build dynamic, robust web applications. Remember that learning Angular is an ongoing process. Practice makes perfect — build your own projects, experiment with the features you learn, and delve into the extensive online resources.

Thank you for joining me in my exploration of Angular. I wish you the best of luck on your programming journey. Have fun programming and good luck with your applications!

Media Attributions

Raising hand concept illustration
Image by storyset on Freepik

Voice message, chat room dialog isometric icon, send
mobile message, smartphone dark neon
Image by fullvector on Freepik

Don't miss out!

Receive an email when Abdelfattah Ragab publishes a new book. It's free and without obligation.

Also by Abdelfattah Ragab

- ◇ Responsive Layouts: Flex, Grid and Multi-Column
- ◇ Angular Portfolio App Development
- ◇ Stripe Integration in Angular
- ◇ Angular HTTP
- ◇ Angular Reactive Forms

About the Author

Abdelfattah Ragab is a professional software developer with more than 20 years of experience.
https://abdelfattah-ragab.com

About the Publisher

Abdelfattah Ragab is a highly qualified and experienced software developer with over 20 years of experience in the industry. Specializing in front-end development, Abdelfattah Ragab has a deep understanding of Angular, JavaScript, TypeScript, HTML and CSS. Read more at https://abdelfattah-ragab.com

www.ingramcontent.com/pod-product-compliance
Lightning Source LLC
LaVergne TN
LVHW041804190726
843493LV00008B/2791